Material Detectives: Glass

Let's Look at Marbles

Angela Royston

Raintree

www.raintreepublishers.co.uk
Visit our website to find out more information about **Raintree** books.

To order:
☎ Phone 44 (0) 1865 888112
▤ Send a fax to 44 (0) 1865 314091
▢ Visit the Raintree Bookshop at **www.raintreepublishers.co.uk** to browse our catalogue and order online.

First published in Great Britain by Raintree, Halley Court, Jordan Hill, Oxford OX2 8EJ, part of Harcourt Education.
Raintree is a registered trademark of Harcourt Education Ltd.

Editorial: Andrew Farrow and Sarah Chappelow
Design: Jo Malivoire and AMR
Picture Research: Erica Newbery
Production: Duncan Gilbert

Originated by Modern Age
Printed and bound in China by South China Printing Company

ISBN 1 844 43427 3 (hardback)
10 09 08 07 06
10 9 8 7 6 5 4 3 2 1

British Library Cataloguing in Publication Data
Royston, Angela
Glass: let's look at marbles – (Material Detectives)
620.1'44
A full catalogue record for this book is available from the British Library

Acknowledgements
The publishers would like to thank the following for permission to reproduce photographs: Myrleen Ferguson Cate/Photo Edit p. **5**; Tudor Photography/Harcourt Education pp. backcover (marble and ball), **4**, **6**, **7**, **8**, **9**, **10**, **11**, **12**, **13**, **14**, **15**, **16**, **17**, **18**, **19**, **20**, **21**, **22**, **23** (all), **24**.

Cover photograph of marbles reproduced with permission of Alamy.

Every effort has been made to contact copyright holders of any material reproduced in this book. Any omissions will be rectified in subsequent printings if notice is given to the publishers.

The paper used to print this book comes from sustainable resources.

Some words are shown in bold, **like this**. They are explained in the glossary on page 23.

Contents

What are marbles?

Marbles are a kind of toy.

You **roll** one along the ground.

Your friends try to hit your marble with theirs.

Are marbles hard or soft?

Marbles are **hard**.

They click when you tap them together.

glass

china

paper

cloth

wood

What do you think marbles are made of?

Marbles are made of glass.

Glass comes in different colours.

Some marbles are see-through.

Others have **hard** coloured pieces inside them.

What shape are marbles?

Marbles are round, like a ball.

You can **roll** marbles across a floor.

Will the marble roll better on the carpet or on the wooden floor?

The marble **rolls** further on the wooden floor.

It rolls faster too.

The carpet is **rough**.

It slows the marble down.

Are marbles rough or smooth?

Marbles are smooth.

You cannot feel any bumps on them.

tangerine

tennis ball

pebble

marble

Which of these things do you think would feel the smoothest?

The marble is the smoothest.

It is so smooth it shines!

The marble is smooth to make it
roll better.

Are marbles light or heavy?

A marble is smaller than a **ping pong** ball.

Which one is **heavier**?

The marble is heavier. It is **solid**.

The ping pong ball is full of air.

How long do marbles last?

Marbles last a long time.

It is not easy to break thick glass.

Marbles do not break when they hit each other.

Marbles are very strong.

Quiz

Which will keep its shape the longest – the marble or the modelling clay?

Look for the answer on page 24.

marble

modelling clay

Glossary

hard
not soft, so you cannot squash it

heavier
weighing more so that it is harder to lift

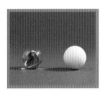

ping pong
table tennis, a game played on a table with
bats and a small ball

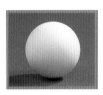

roll
move by turning over and over

rough
uneven and bumpy

Index

Answer to the quiz question on page 22

The marble will keep its shape the longest. The modelling clay is soft and will soon lose its shape.

Note to parents and teachers

Reading for information is an important part of a child's literacy development. Learning begins with a question about something. Help children think of themselves as investigators and researchers by encouraging their questions about the world around them. Each chapter in this book begins with a question. Read the question together. Look at the pictures. Talk about what you think the answer might be. Then read the text to find out if your predictions were correct. Think of other questions you could ask about the topic, and discuss where you might find the answers. Assist children in using the picture glossary and the index to practice new vocabulary and research skills.

Titles in the *Material Detectives* series include:

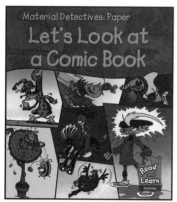

Material Detectives: Paper
Let's Look at a Comic Book

Hardback   1 844 43429 X

Material Detectives: Plastic
Let's Look at the Frisbee®

Hardback   1 844 43430 3

Material Detectives: Soil
Let's Look at a Garden

Hardback   1 844 43636 5

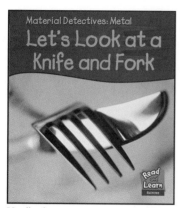

Material Detectives: Metal
Let's Look at a Knife and Fork

Hardback   1 844 43428 1

Material Detectives: Glass
Let's Look at Marbles

Hardback   1 844 43427 3

Material Detectives: Rock
Let's Look at Pebbles

Hardback   1 844 43634 9

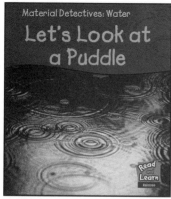

Material Detectives: Water
Let's Look at a Puddle

Hardback   1 844 43635 7

Material Detectives: Wood
Let's Look at a Sports Bat

Hardback   1 844 43637 3

Find out about other titles from Raintree on our website www.raintreepublishers.co.uk